Anatomy & P #1

Bones Muscles and The Stuff That Connects Bones and Muscles

MW01152087

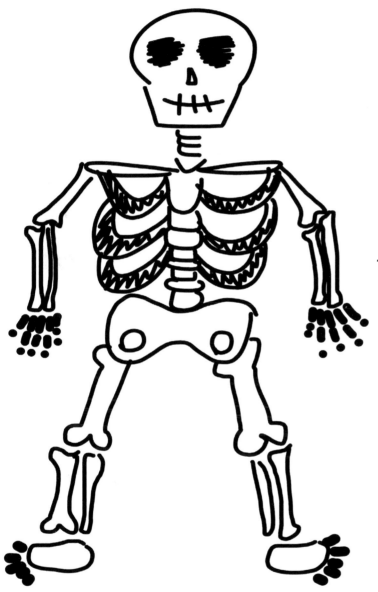

This book is dedicated to my Mom & Dad, Kim and Joel Terrazas.

Thank you so much for your wholehearted support of all of my endeavors since early childhood!

By: April Chloe Terrazas

Anatomy & Physiology PART 1: Bones, Muscles, and The Stuff That Connects Bones and Muscles.
April Chloe Terrazas, BS University of Texas at Austin.
Copyright © 2014 Crazy Brainz, LLC

Visit us on the web! www.Crazy-Brainz.com

Anatomy art competition winners:
Taj Estrada and Sydney Estrada!

Congratulations!
We LOVE your portrayal of human anatomy!

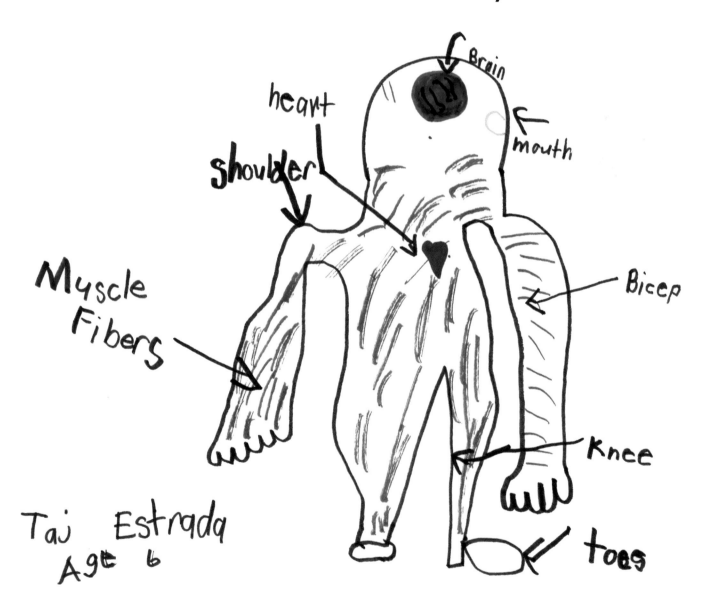

The Inside of a Bone

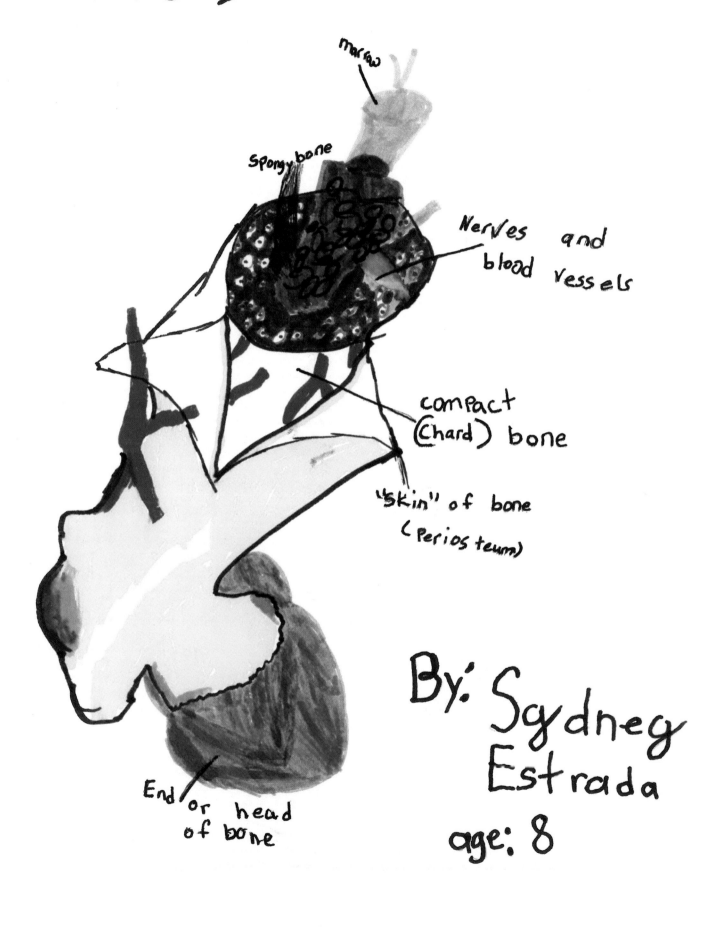

marow

Spongy bone

Nerves and blood vessels

compact (hard) bone

"skin" of bone (Periosteum)

End or head of bone

By: Sydney Estrada
age: 8

Anatomy

Sound it Out
1. UH
2. NA
3. TO
4. ME

Physiology

Sound it Out
1. FIZ
2. E
3. OL
4. O
5. JEE

Anatomy is the structure of a living organism *(how it looks)*. For example, the hand is small with fingers on it.

Physiology is the function of a living organism, *(how it works)*. For example, the hand moves to write or play an instrument.

What is the **anatomy**
of your face?

How does it look?

Eyes
Nose
Mouth

What is the physiology
of your face?

How does it work?

See
Smell
Talk
Eat

Bone

Sound it Out

1. BONE

Skeleton

Sound it Out

1. SKEL
2. EH
3. TUN

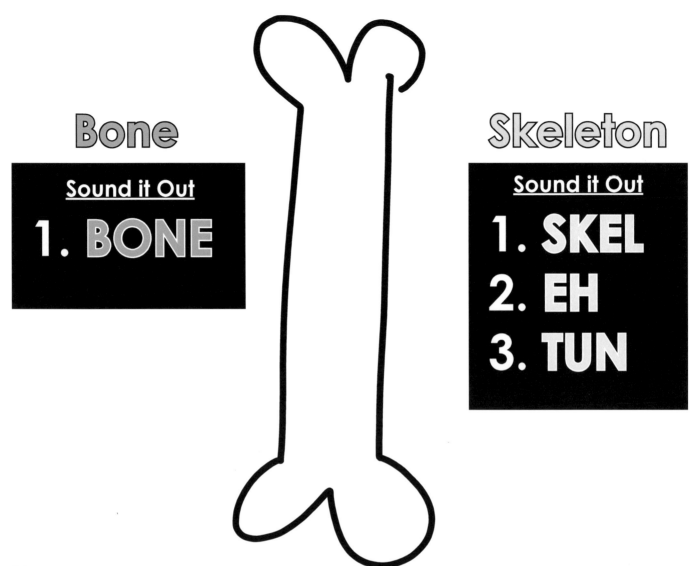

Bones are hard tissue that make up the skeleton. Without bones, we would be like a ball of jelly!

Bones are alive and can grow and change shape.

A human adult has 206 bones!

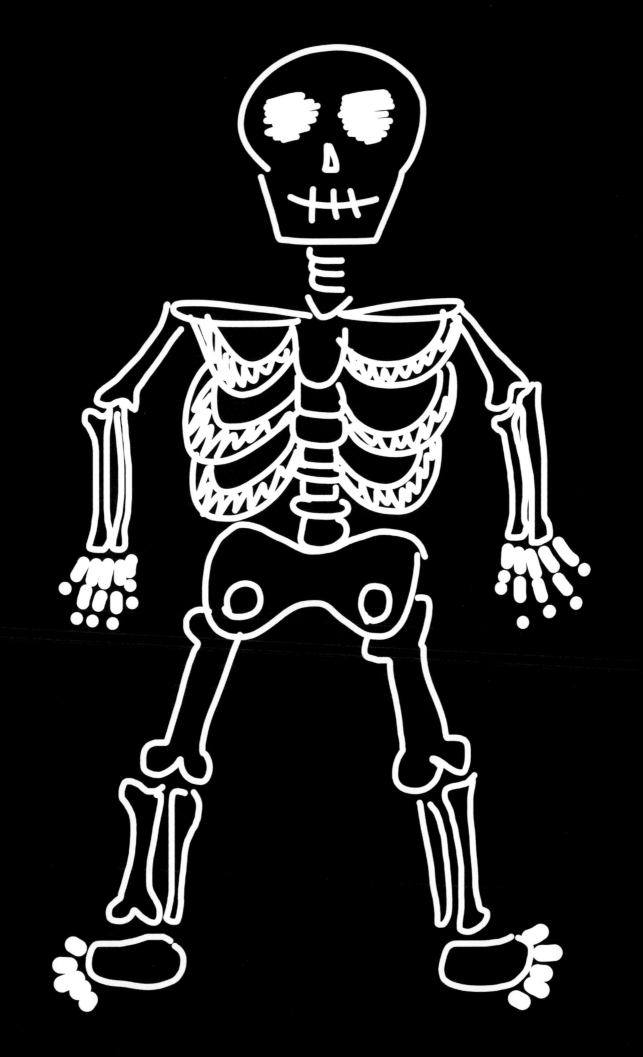

This is a <u>long bone</u>.
<u>Long bones</u> are in your legs, arms and even your fingers!

The epiphysis is the end of a <u>long bone</u>.

The diaphysis is the shaft of a <u>long bone</u>.

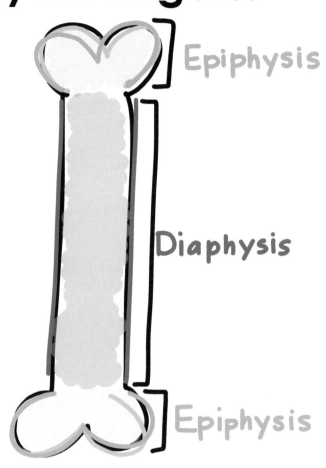

Epiphysis

Diaphysis

Epiphysis

Epiphysis

Sound it Out

1. E
2. PIF
3. EH
4. SUS

Diaphysis

Sound it Out

1. DI
2. AF
3. EH
4. SUS

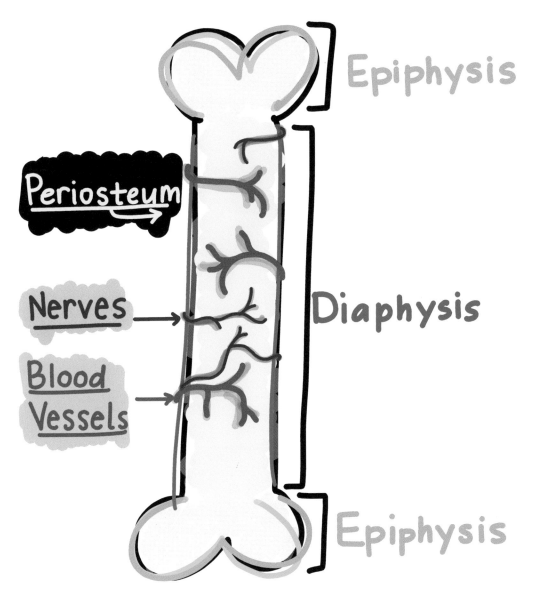

Epiphysis

Periosteum →

Nerves →

Blood Vessels →

Diaphysis

Epiphysis

Periosteum is a membrane that covers the outer surface of bones and has nerves and blood vessels.

Periosteum

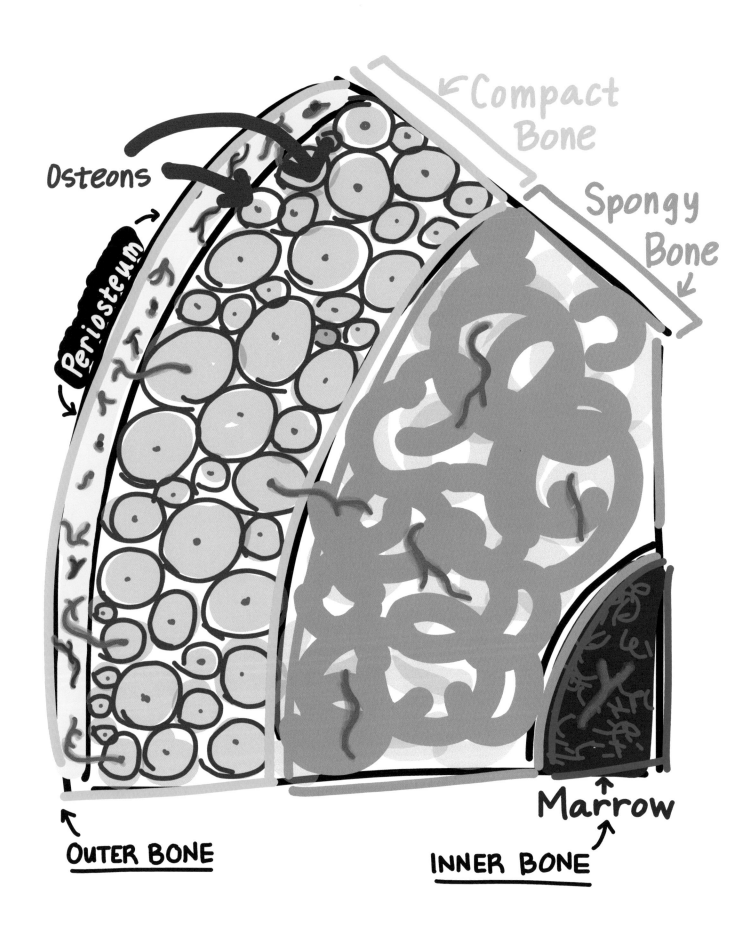

Osteons

Periosteum

OUTER BONE

Compact Bone

Spongy Bone

Marrow

INNER BONE

(Inside a bone)

The outer layer of the bone is called compact bone.

Compact bone is made of osteons and periosteum.

Osteons are layers of dense bone with a canal inside for blood vessels.

Do you see the red blood vessels inside the osteons?

Osteon

Compact Bone

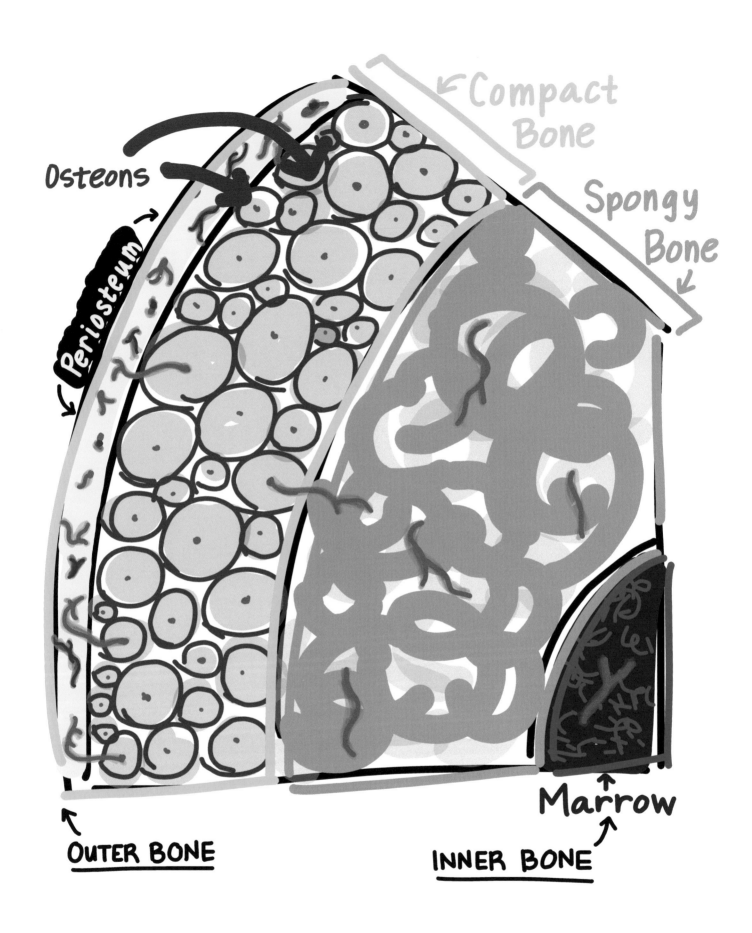

Osteons

Periosteum

Compact Bone

Spongy Bone

Marrow

OUTER BONE

INNER BONE

(Inside a bone)

The inner layer (the middle) of the **bone** is made of **marrow** and **spongy bone**.

Marrow is a soft substance that fills the spongy bone and makes blood cells.

*What are **osteons**?*
What is compact bone made of?
What is periosteum?

Spongy Bone

Marrow

Sound it Out
1. MER
2. O

Sound it Out
1. SPUN
2. JEE
1. BONE

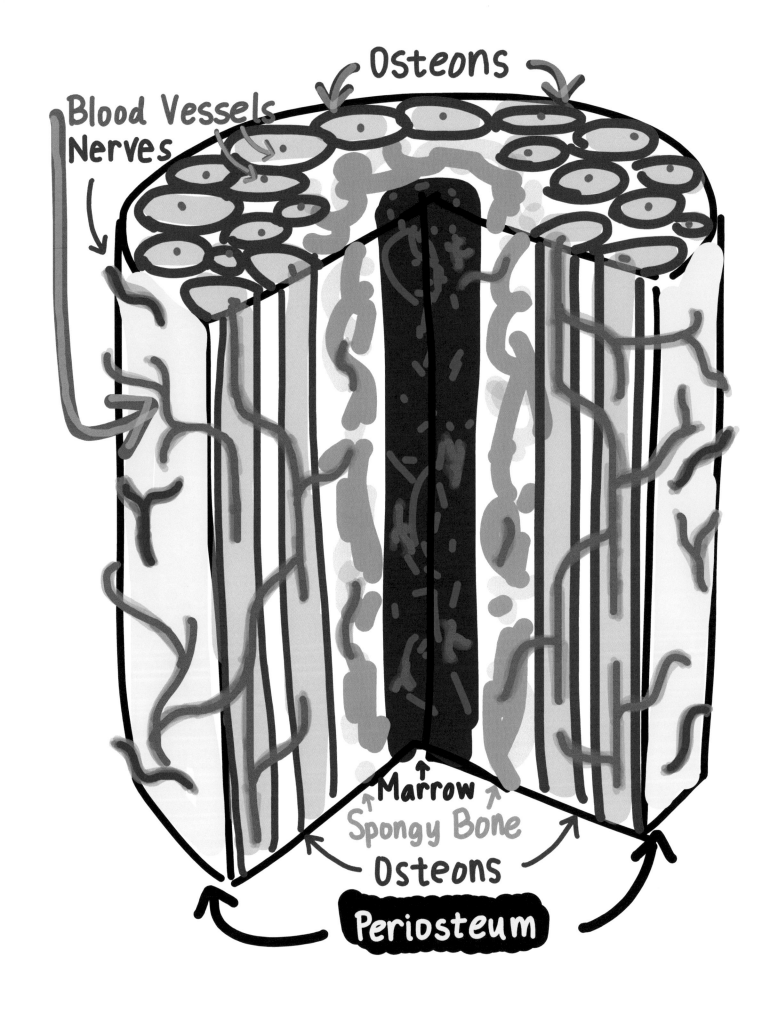

Osteons

Blood Vessels
Nerves

Marrow
Spongy Bone
Osteons
Periosteum

Starting from the middle of the bone going outward:

Marrow

Spongy Bone

Osteons

Periosteum

Blood vessels go from the outer membrane of the periosteum into the bone!

This is how your bone heals when it is fractured or broken.

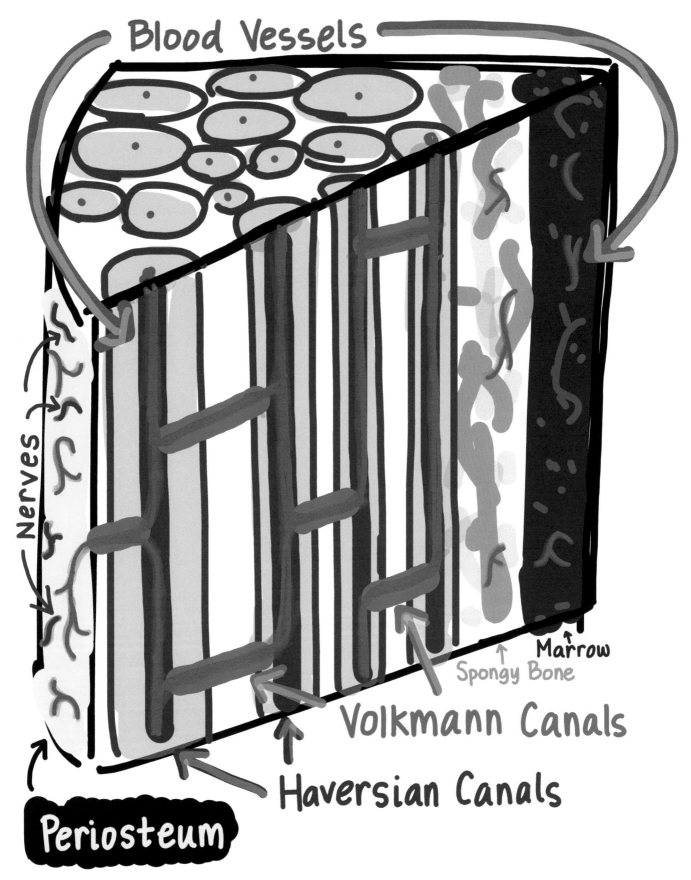

Blood vessels **are located**
in the canals of the osteons.

The canals inside the **osteons** are called **Haversian Canals**. They go *up and down*.

Haversian Canal

Sound it Out

1. HUH
2. VER
3. SHUN

1. KUH
2. NAL

Volkmann Canal

Sound it Out

1. VOLK
2. MUN

1. KUH
2. NAL

The **blood vessels** move from *side to side* between **osteons** through Volkmann canals.

Volkmann canals also connect the outer periosteum to the inner **osteons**.

The outer compact bone is made of periosteum and osteons.

The inner bone is made of marrow inside spongy bone.

Blood vessels go from the outer periosteum to the osteons through volkmann canals that go from *side to side*.

Blood vessels move *up and down* the osteons through haversian canals.

Blood vessels inside the bone are the way fractured or broken bones heal.

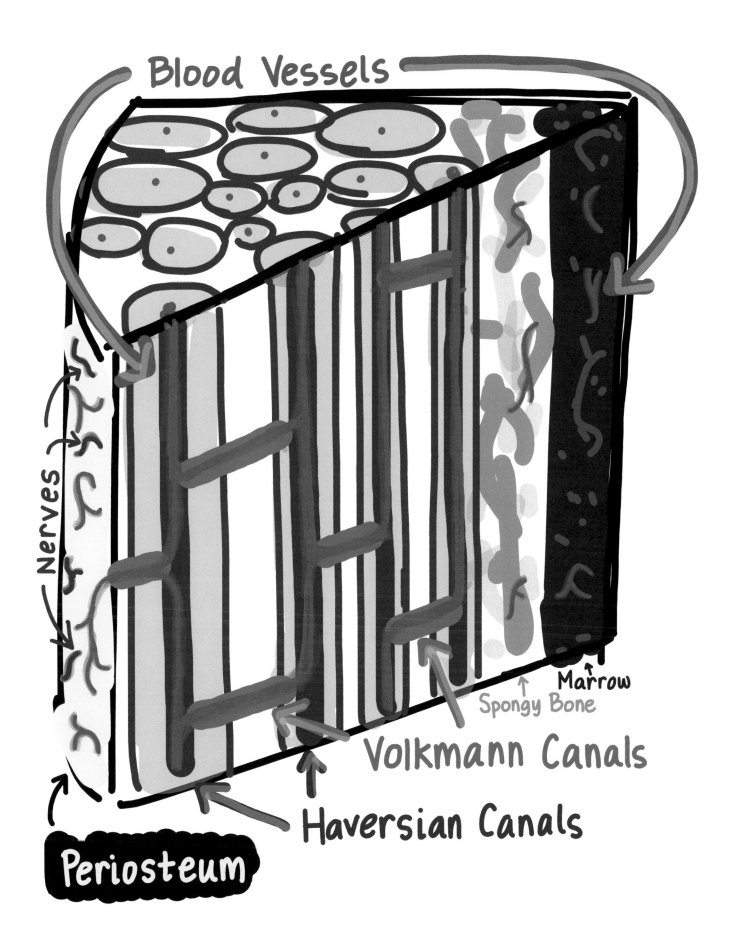

Blood Vessels

Nerves

Periosteum

Haversian Canals

Volkmann Canals

Spongy Bone

Marrow

What is the periosteum?

What is the difference between the **haversian canals** and the volkmann canals?

What is compact bone?

What is the difference between the epiphysis and **diaphysis**?

CONGRATULATIONS!

You are now a
*bone **anatomy** expert!*

MUSCLE

There are 3 types of muscle in your body:

Skeletal
SKEL-EH-TUL

Cardiac
KAR-DEE-AK

Smooth
SMOOTH

Skeletal muscles are <u>voluntary</u> muscles. This means that <u>you</u> <u>control</u> the movement.

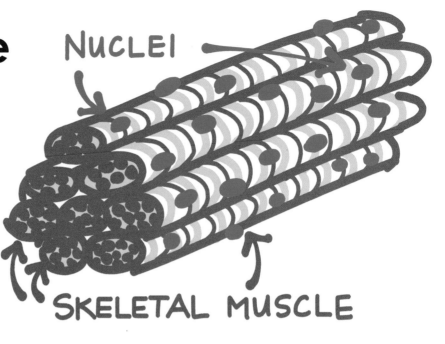

NUCLEI

SKELETAL MUSCLE

Skeletal muscles are striated. Striated means striped.

Do you see the striated skeletal muscle?

Skeletal muscles work together with the skeleton to move your body.

Striated

Sound it Out

1. STRI
2. A
3. TED

Skeletal muscles are attached to bones by tendons.

Tendons are made of white fiber-like tissue.

Tendon

Sound it Out

1. TEN
2. DUN

Tendons are VERY strong. They have to be because they hold the skeleton together.

How many bones are in a human skeleton?

Tendons allow you to run, walk, jump, lift and dance.

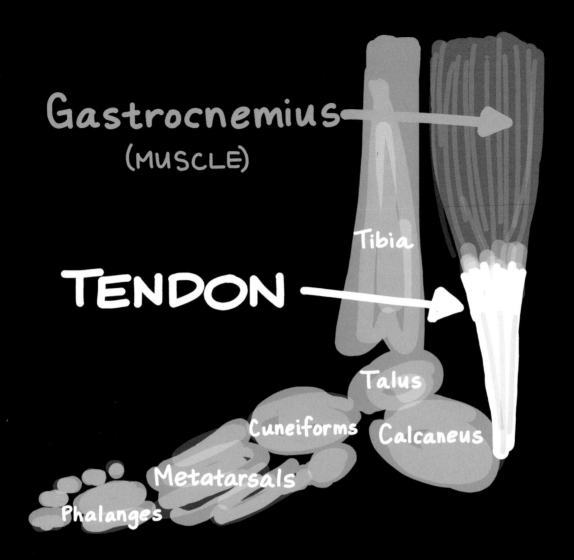

Gastrocnemius
(MUSCLE)

Tibia

TENDON

Talus

Cuneiforms

Calcaneus

Metatarsals

Phalanges

Gastrocnemius

This is a tendon that connects the heel to the gastrocnemius muscle so you can run and jump!

Sound it Out

1. GAS
2. TROK
3. NEE
4. MEE
5. US

Say the names of the bones in the lower leg and foot.

Tibia = TIB-EE-UH

Talus = TAL-US

Cuneiforms = Q-NEE-UH-FORMS

Calcaneus = KAL-KAN-EE-US

Metatarsals = MET-UH-TAR-SULS

Phalanges = FUH-LAN-JEES

The tendon connects
the **calcaneus** bone to the
gastrocnemius (skeletal) muscle.

Tendons connect muscle to bone.

Ligaments connect bone to bone.

Ligament

Sound it Out
1. LIG
2. UH
3. MENT

Ligaments connect the femur (thigh bone) to the tibia (shin bone) at the knee joint.

Cartilage is in your joints, ears, nose and throat!

Cartilage

Sound it Out
1. KAR
2. TEH
3. LEJ

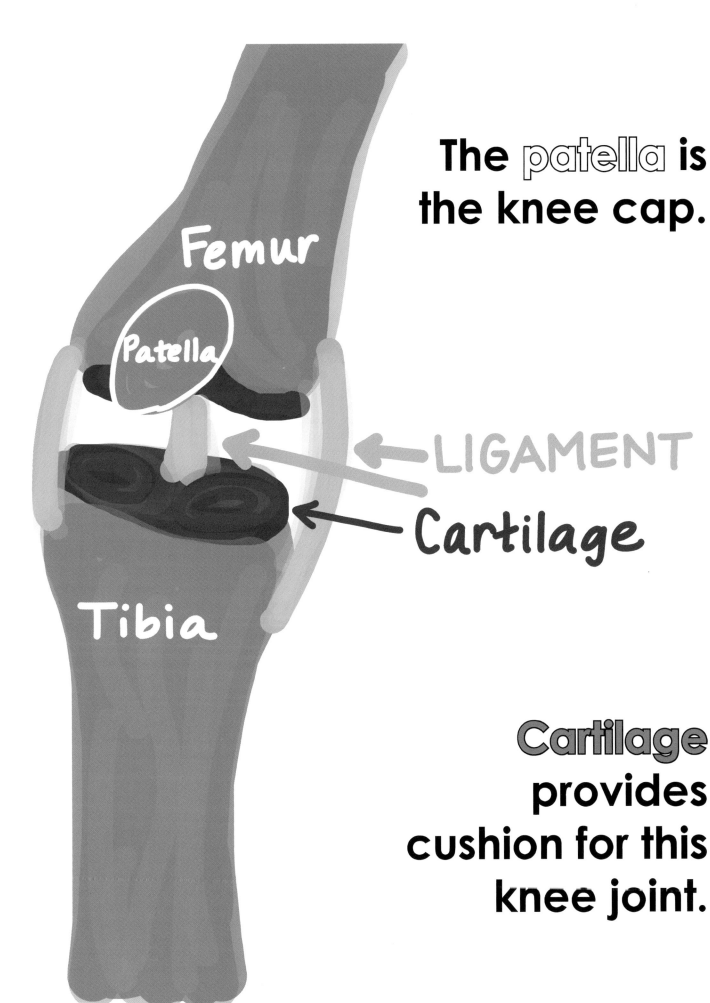

The **patella** is the knee cap.

Cartilage provides cushion for this knee joint.

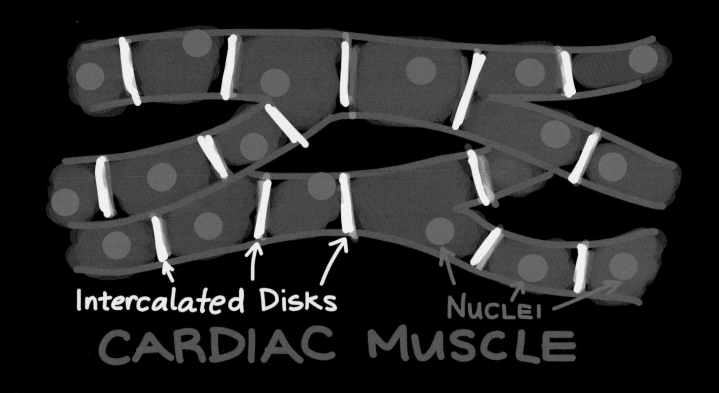

Intercalated Disks

Nuclei

CARDIAC MUSCLE

Cardiac muscle is <u>involuntary</u>.

<u>You do not control</u>
your heart beat.

Cardiac muscle does not get tired. Cardiac muscle contracts to push blood out of the heart and relaxes to draw blood into the heart.

joined at intercalated disks.

Intercalated disks create the striations in cardiac muscle.

Intercalated

Disks

Sound it Out

1. IN
2. TER
3. KUH
4. LA
5. TED

Sound it Out

1. DSKS

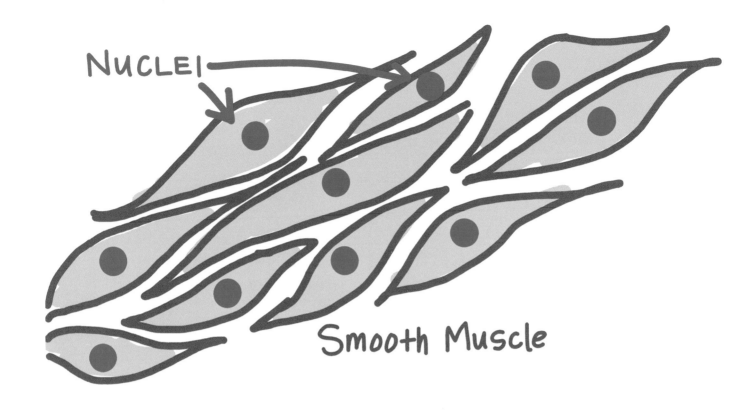

NUCLEI

Smooth Muscle

Smooth muscle is <u>involuntary</u>, it works automatically in your body.

Smooth muscle is in your stomach, intestines and even in your eye!

REVIEW:
Skeletal muscle is <u>voluntary</u>, striated and it is found all over your body.

Skeletal muscle connects to bones through tendons, like the calcaneus to the gastrocnemius.

Ligaments connect bone to bone, like the femur to the tibia.

Cardiac muscle is <u>involuntary</u> and found only in the heart.

Intercalated disks make the striations in cardiac muscle.

Smooth muscle is <u>involuntary</u> and found in your eye.

We know what bones and muscles look like, we know their anatomy. But how do our bones and muscles move?

When the muscle moves, the bones move because bones are connected to muscle through tendons.

What makes our muscles move?

The brain!

Neurons carry messages from our brain to our muscles.

(Review the structure and function of the neuron in Neurology: The Amazing Central Nervous System - book 3 of the Series - and elements in Chemistry: The Atom and Elements - book 2 of the Series)

The message to move is sent from the brain, through the neurons, to the muscle.

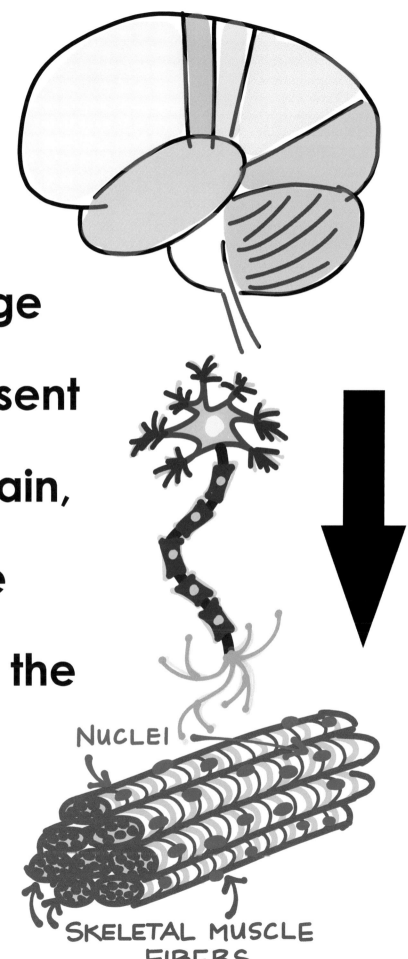

NUCLEI

SKELETAL MUSCLE FIBERS

Axon Terminal

We are going to look
at how the message is sent
from the neuron to the muscle.

This happens at the
Neuromuscular Junction.

Sound it Out
1. NUR
2. O
3. MUS
4. KU
5. LER

Sound it Out
1. JUNK
2. SHUN

(A junction is a
meeting place)

The neuromuscular junction
involves this part of the neuron,
called the axon terminal,
communicating with the
muscle fibers.

Some super cool terms to know before we begin:

Calcium (Ca^{2+})
KAL-SEE-UM

Acetylcholine (ACh)
UH-SEE-TiL-KO-LEEN

Receptor
REE-SEP-TER

Synaptic vesicle
SIN-AP-TIK   VES-EH-KL

Sarcolemma
SAR-KO-LEM-UH

Neuromuscular Junction

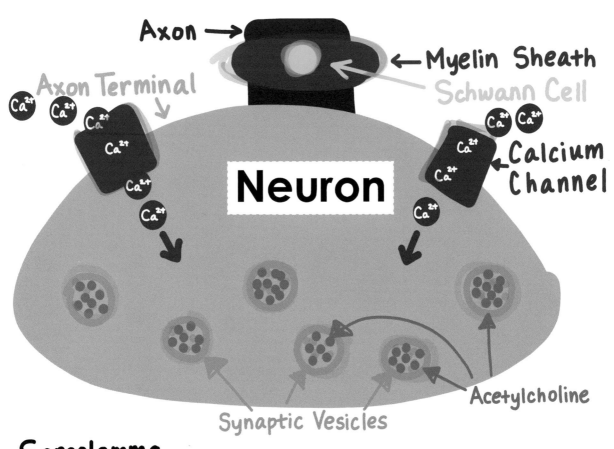

Axon →

← Myelin Sheath

Schwann Cell

Axon Terminal

Ca²⁺ Ca²⁺ Ca²⁺ Ca²⁺ Ca²⁺ Ca²⁺

Neuron

Ca²⁺ Ca²⁺ Ca²⁺ Ca²⁺ Ca²⁺

← Calcium Channel

Acetylcholine

Synaptic Vesicles

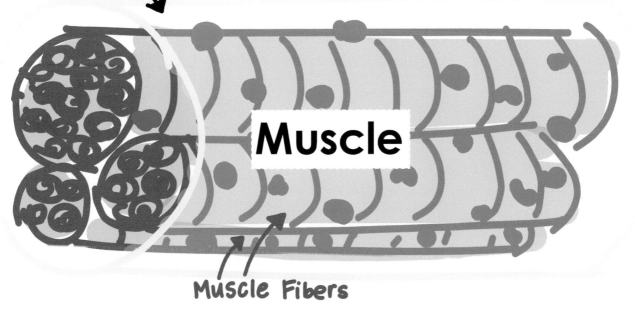

Sarcolemma

Muscle

Muscle Fibers

When the message reaches the axon terminal, it allows the element calcium (Ca^{2+}) to enter into the axon terminal.

The entry of calcium (Ca^{2+}) into the axon terminal causes the synaptic vesicles to come out of the axon terminal.

When the synaptic vesicles open, they release acetylcholine (ACh) into the space between the neuron and the sarcolemma (the membrane around the muscle fibers).

Neuromuscular Junction

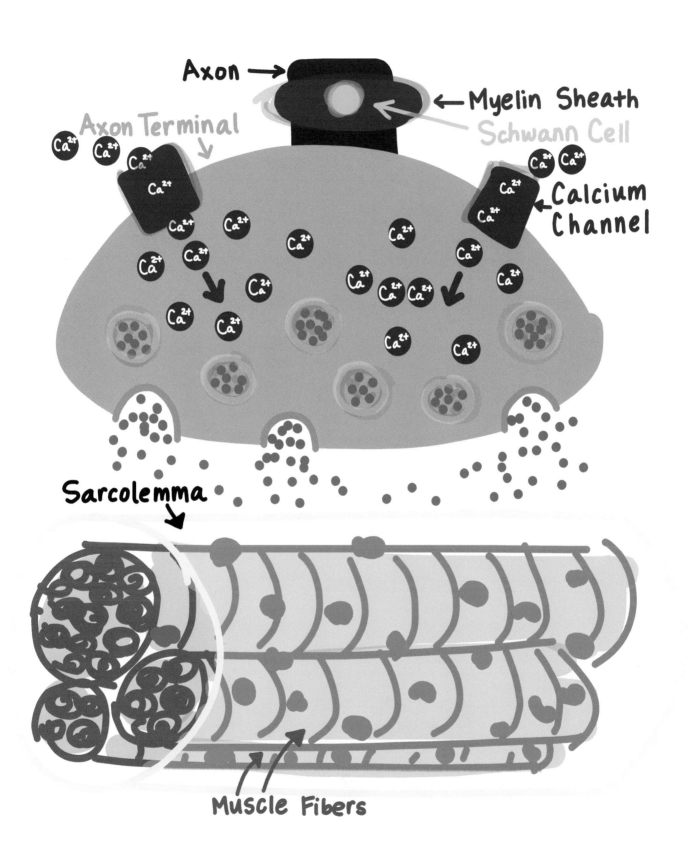

Next, **acetylcholine (ACh)** binds to the **ACh** receptors on the sarcolemma.

Review:
The message allows **calcium** into the axon terminal which causes the synaptic vesicles to release **acetylcholine** into the space between the neuron and the sarcolemma.
Then, **ACh** binds to the **ACh** receptors on the sarcolemma.

What is the sarcolemma?
What is the name of this junction where the neuron and muscle fiber meet?

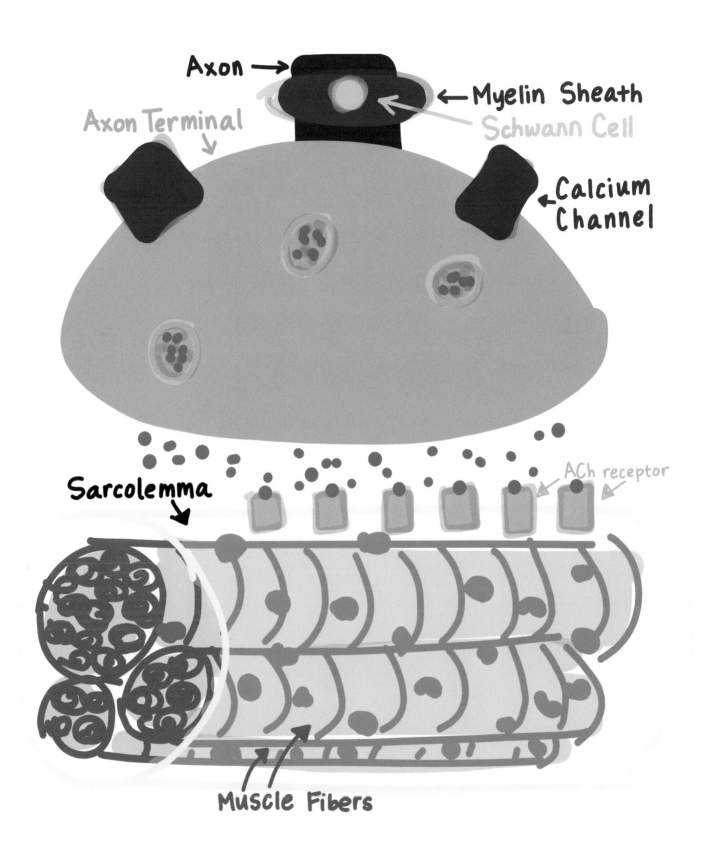

After **ACh** binds to the **ACh** receptor, it allows the element **sodium (Na⁺)** to enter into the sarcolemma.

When enough **sodium (Na⁺)** enters the sarcolemma, the muscle is able to contract!

Brain

↓

Neuron

↓

Neuromuscular Junction

↓

Muscle

↓

CONTRACTION!

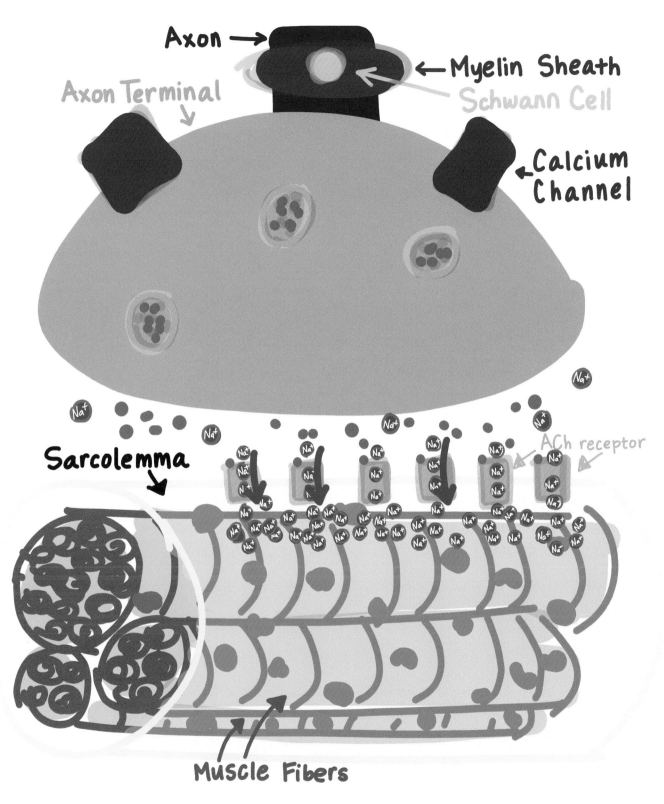

Sodium enters the sarcolemma, causing the muscle to contract.

A human adult has 206 bones.

The epiphysis is the end of a long bone, the diaphysis is the shaft of a long bone.

The outer compact bone is made of osteons and periosteum.

The inner bone is made of spongy bone and marrow.

Haversian canals go *up and down.* Volkmann canals go *side to side.*

Skeletal muscle is voluntary and striated. Skeletal muscles are attached to bones by tendons. Cartilage provides structure and cushion in your joints and nose.

Ligaments connect bone to bone.

Cardiac muscle is <u>involuntary</u> and striated from intercalated disks. (ONLY in the heart).

Smooth muscle is <u>involuntary</u> and automatic. (Stomach, eyes).

Movement in our body is starts with a message from the brain that travels through neurons to the muscle. The message causes **calcium (Ca^{2+})** to enter into the axon terminal, which signals **acetylcholine** to be released from the synaptic vesicles of the neuron and bind to the **ACh** receptors on the sarcolemma of the muscle, which allows **sodium (Na^+)** to enter and cause contraction of the muscle.

New Vocabulary!

Anatomy	Spongy Bone
Physiology	**Haversian Canal**
Bone	Volkmann Canal
Skeleton	Skeletal muscle
Epiphysis	Cardiac muscle
Diaphysis	Smooth muscle
Periosteum	**Striated**
Compact Bone	**Tendon**
Osteon	Gastrocnemius
Marrow	

Cartilage

Tibia

Talus

Cuneiforms

Calcaneus

Metatarsals

Phalanges

Ligament

Patella

<u>Voluntary</u>

<u>Involuntary</u>

Intercalated Disk

Neuromuscular Junction

Axon Terminal

Calcium (Ca^{2+})

Acetylcholine (ACh)

Receptor

Synaptic Vesicle

Sarcolemma

Sodium (Na$^+$)

You are a bone, muscle, and neurology expert!

The Super Smart Science Series for ages 0-100:

#1 - Cellular Biology
Organelles, Structure, Function

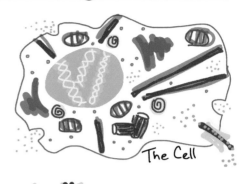

The Cell

#2 - Chemistry
The Atom and Elements

#3 - Neurology
The Amazing Central Nervous System

#4 - Astronomy
The Solar System

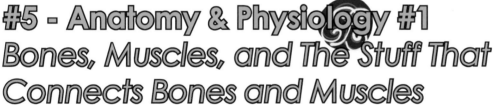

#5 - Anatomy & Physiology #1
Bones, Muscles, and The Stuff That Connects Bones and Muscles

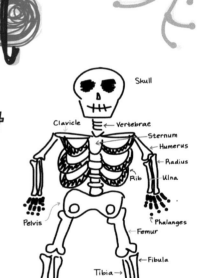

#6 - Anatomy & Physiology #2
Body Systems

#7 - Cardiology
The Incredible Heart

...and more!
www.SuperSmartScienceSeries.com

Draw YOUR bones, muscles, ligaments, tendons, neurons and label the parts!

CPSIA information can be obtained at www.ICGtesting.com
Printed in the USA
LVIW01n1522050617
536981LV00012B/155